Welcome to the Joy of Christmas Crafting!

The holiday season is a magical time filled with love, laughter, and the joy of giving. It's the perfect opportunity to bring your creative spirit to life and fill your home with the warmth of handmade treasures. Whether you're crafting gifts for loved ones, decorating your home with festive flair, or wrapping presents with a personal touch, this book is your guide to making Christmas extra special this year.

Inside these pages, you'll find a collection of delightful and inspiring projects designed to suit all ages and skill levels. From whimsical ornaments and cozy decorations to heartfelt gifts and charming wrapping ideas, every craft is an opportunity to create memories and share the magic of the season with family and friends.

Crafting isn't just about the final product—it's about the process, the shared moments, and the stories you create along the way. So, grab your scissors, glue, and glitter, and let's embark on a journey of creativity, joy, and festive cheer.

No matter you're crafting experience, you'll discover something here to spark your imagination and bring a little more sparkle to your holidays. Let's make this Christmas the most memorable one yet— filled with love, laughter, and handmade magic.
Happy crafting, and may your holiday season be merry and bright!
Warm wishes,
Ryan

Ornaments and Tree Decorations

1. Rustic Cinnamon Stick Stars

Materials: Cinnamon sticks, hot glue, twine, small pine sprigs, or mini holly berries.

Instructions: Arrange five cinnamon sticks in a star shape, securing the points with hot glue. Add small pine sprigs or holly berries at the intersections for a festive touch. Attach a loop of twine for hanging.

2. Personalized Wood Slice Ornaments

Materials: Small wood slices, acrylic paint or paint pens, glitter, ribbon.

Instructions: Paint or write family members' names, initials, or Christmas designs on each wood slice. Add glitter accents and tie a ribbon through a small hole drilled at the top for hanging.

3. Snowy Pine cone Ornaments

Materials: Pine cones, white acrylic paint, small paintbrush, twine, mini bells (optional).

Instructions: Lightly dab the edges of pine cone scales with white paint to mimic snow. Once dry, attach twine around the top for hanging and add mini bells if desired.

4. Salt Dough Ornaments

Materials: Salt dough (made from flour, salt, and water), cookie cutters, acrylic paint, ribbon.

Instructions: Roll out the dough and use cookie cutters to create holiday shapes. Use a straw to make a hole for the ribbon. Bake, then paint and decorate. Thread ribbon through the hole for hanging.

5. Mini Wreath Ornaments

Materials: Mini wreath bases (or make your own with wire), faux greenery, mini pine cones, red ribbon.

Instructions: Wrap faux greenery around the wreath base and add mini pine cones with hot glue. Finish with a red ribbon tied in a bow and a loop for hanging.

6. Felt Reindeer Faces

Materials: Brown, red, and black felt, googly eyes, craft glue, scissors.

Instructions: Cut out a brown circle for the face, add small felt pieces for ears, and a red nose. Attach googly eyes and add a loop on the back for hanging.

HOME DECOR

1. Natural Evergreen Wreath

Materials: Evergreen branches, wire wreath frame, floral wire, pine cones, red ribbon, small ornaments (optional).

Instructions: Attach the evergreen branches to the wreath frame using floral wire, layering for fullness. Add pine cones and small ornaments for extra decoration, then finish with a big red ribbon. Hang on the front door or above the fireplace.

2. Mason Jar Snowy candleholders

Materials: Mason jars, white paint or Epsom salt, mod podge, tea lights, twine, small pine sprigs

Instructions: Paint the outside of the jars white or apply mod podge and roll in Epsom salt for a frosty look. Tie twine around the top with a small pine sprig. Place a tea light inside to create a cozy, snow-kissed glow.

3. Holiday Table Centerpiece

Materials: Wooden tray, small evergreen branches, pine cones, mini ornaments, pillar candles, faux snow.

Instructions: Arrange pillar candles in the center of the tray, surrounding them with small branches, pine cones, and mini ornaments. Sprinkle faux snow over everything for a wintery feel. This makes a festive and elegant centerpiece for the dining table.

4. DIY Garland with Dried Oranges and Cinnamon Sticks

Materials: Dried orange slices, cinnamon sticks, twine, evergreen sprigs, small ornaments (optional).

Instructions: Thread twine through dried orange slices and attach cinnamon sticks, alternating with small evergreen sprigs or ornaments. Drape across a mantel or along a banister for a naturally fragrant, rustic garland.

5. Wine Bottle Christmas Lights

Materials: Empty wine bottles, string lights (battery-operated), holiday ribbon.

Instructions: Place a strand of string lights inside each wine bottle, leaving the battery pack outside. Wrap holiday ribbon around the neck of each bottle. Line them up along a windowsill or table for a festive glow.

6. Snowman Stacked Flower Pots

Materials: Three small terracotta flower pots, white paint, black buttons, orange and black paint, twine, small hat (optional).

Instructions: Paint the pots white, then stack them upside-down to form a snowman. Paint a face on the top pot and add buttons down the middle pot. Tie twine around the "neck" for a scarf and add a small hat on top.

7. DIY Christmas Door Hanging Basket

Materials: Woven basket with a handle, faux greenery, red berries, pine cones, ribbon.

Instructions: Fill the basket with faux greenery, berries, and pine cones. Add a festive ribbon on the handle, then hang it on the door as an alternative to a traditional wreath.

8. Wooden Tree Slice Table Coasters

Materials: Small wood slices, holiday-themed stamps or paint, varnish.

Instructions: Stamp or paint each wood slice with a holiday design (snowflakes, trees, stars). Let dry, then seal with varnish to protect the design. These make great holiday coasters for festive gatherings.

9. Paper Star Window Hangings

Materials: Craft paper, scissors, glue, twine.

Instructions: Fold and cut craft paper into star shapes, then glue multiple stars together for a layered look. Add twine and hang them in the windows for a delicate and festive touch.

10. Festive Throw Pillow Covers

Materials: Plain pillow covers, holiday-themed stencils, fabric paint.

Instructions: Use stencils to paint holiday designs onto plain pillow covers (think snowflakes, reindeer, or "Merry Christmas" text). Let dry, then add to your couch or chairs for a cozy holiday look.

GIFTS AND WRAPPING

1. Painted Mugs

Materials: Plain ceramic mugs, oil-based paint pens, oven.

Instructions: Use paint pens to create festive designs or personalized messages on the mugs. Let the paint dry, then bake the mugs at 350°F (175°C) for 30 minutes to set the paint. Perfect for hot cocoa lovers!

2. Scented Soy Candles

Materials: Soy wax flakes, essential oils, wicks, mason jars, ribbon.

Instructions: Melt soy wax, mix in a few drops of essential oil, and pour into mason jars with a wick centered inside. Let cool and set, then decorate the jar with ribbon or a holiday tag.

3. DIY Bath Bombs

Materials: Baking soda, citric acid, Epsom salt, essential oils, molds.

Instructions: Mix ingredients in a bowl, press into molds, and let dry overnight. Package in clear cellophane with a ribbon and gift tag.

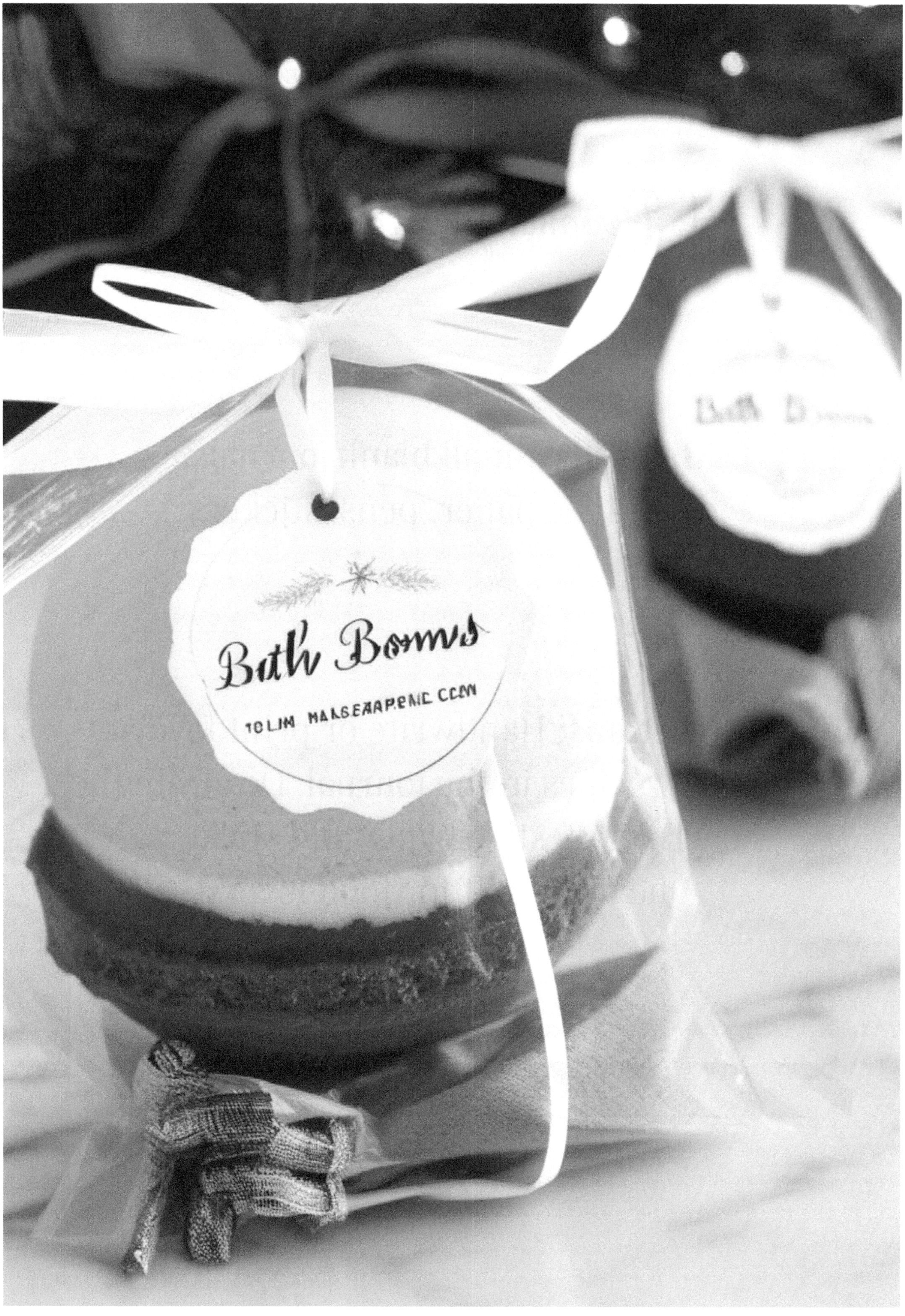
Bath Bomvs

4. Personalized Recipe Books

Materials: Small blank journals, decorative paper, pens, stickers.

Instructions: Handwrite or print favorite holiday recipes in the journal. Decorate the cover with festive paper and stickers. A heartfelt gift for food lovers!

5. Kraft Paper Wrapping

Materials: Brown Kraft paper, twine, stamps, and ink.

Instructions: Wrap gifts in Kraft paper and tie with twine. Use holiday-themed stamps (snowflakes, trees) to decorate the paper. Add sprigs of greenery or cinnamon sticks for a rustic touch.

6. Fabric Gift Wrap (Furoshiki Style)

Materials: Holiday-themed fabric squares.

Instructions: Use fabric to wrap gifts by folding and knotting the edges in creative ways. Add a small ornament or candy cane for embellishment.

7. DIY Gift Bags

Materials: Plain paper bags, markers, stickers, ribbons.

Instructions: Decorate plain bags with festive doodles or stickers. Use ribbon to create handles or to tie the top closed.

8. Recycled Wrapping

Materials: Old maps, sheet music, newspaper, twine.

Instructions: Use recycled materials as gift wrap and tie with natural twine. Add handwritten tags for a unique touch.

Gift Toppers

1. Mini Ornaments

Materials: Small ornaments, ribbon.

Instructions: Attach a mini ornament to the ribbon on wrapped gifts for an extra special touch.

2.DIY Clay Tags

Materials: Air-dry
clay, cookie cutters,
stamps.

Instructions: Roll out clay, cut
into shapes with cookie cutters,
and stamp with designs or names.
Let dry and tie to gifts with
ribbon.

Last–Minute Gifts

Hot Cocoa Kits

Materials: Mason jars, hot cocoa mix, mini marshmallows, chocolate chips, candy canes.

Instructions: Layer hot cocoa mix, marshmallows, and chocolate chips in a jar. Tie with a ribbon and include a candy cane for stirring.

Cookie Mix Jars

Materials: Mason jars, cookie ingredients (layered), ribbon, printable recipe cards.

Instructions: Layer dry cookie ingredients in a jar, add a festive ribbon, and attach a recipe card with instructions.

Made in the USA
Monee, IL
15 December 2024

73690832R00044